OLYMPIC WEIGHTLIFTING

CUES & CORRECTIONS

DANIEL CAMARGO

ISBN-13: 978-0-9907985-0-7

APOD

Catalyst Athletics, Inc.
www.catalystathletics.com

OLYMPIC WEIGHTLIFTING

CUES & CORRECTIONS

DANIEL CAMARGO

Dedicated to the man who shaped my athletic career and my coaching career, Bill "Coach Mac" McDaniel. May you always rest in peace.

ACKNOWLEDGMENTS

It would be very hard for me to have written this book without acknowledging the many people who have molded my Olympic Weightlifting experience to this day. After 24 years involved with the movements, I am still being molded and I meet people every day who in some way influence my path. Though this book is an accomplishment for me, my journey isn't over and I embrace the fact that my weightlifting life has no destination. It's a journey I'll continue forever.

I'll start with my parents, Orlando Camargo Sr. & Tina Camargo, who allowed me to be a weightlifter as a young boy. See, I competed in a sport that was very unpopular and misunderstood. My parents are from the generation that believed youth weight training was dangerous. They were made to believe that it would stunt a child's growth and that injury was prevalent. Yet, they supported me and gave me permission to compete in Olympic weightlifting. It made me happy and they saw it kept me focused, out of trouble, and the opportunities were growing, albeit smaller in comparison to more popular sports such as football, baseball, or gymnastics. They couldn't have known then that their trust and support would lead me where I have been nor that it would shape decisions in my life that have proven beneficial. You wouldn't be reading this book had it not been for my parents. So I owe it all to them.

Next, I'll recognize my coaches. At the age of 12 I was introduced to the sport by my first coach and mentor, Bill "Coach Mac" McDaniel. He developed me into a junior elite weightlifter and I realize much of my coaching style has come from him. By the age of 16 I had an opportunity to move away from home and train full time for the Olympics at the United States Olympic Training Center in Colorado Springs, CO. In my three-and-a-half-year tenure, my primary coach was the then national coach, Dragomir Cioroslan. My programming style and vocal presence with my athletes has certainly been influenced by him. I was also coached by the assistant, Bob Morris, whose ability to know our limits better then ourselves still baffles me to this day. As is customary in weightlifting, an athlete's routine coaches, in my case Coach Mac, Dragomir, and Bob (yes, they were all known by first name), would not be present at some international events I competed in. There was, as there is today, a selection process, and though these men were high level coaches, they weren't always at my tournaments. Those who were, were also great coaches such as Mike Burgener, Leo Totten, Mike Cohen, Mike Conroy, and a man who always believed in me, John Thrush. All of these coaches had some impact on my athletic career and in many ways have influenced my coaching profession.

After my retirement at the age of 21, early in the eyes of many, I took a short period of time away but came right back to the sport I loved. I have to thank my very first athlete Leigh Francis, who pestered me to get back in the gym. Though I wasn't ready for the responsibility, it was Leigh who wouldn't give up until I coached him. As soon as I did, I realized my calling and he and I have remained close friends well after his departure as an athlete. I couldn't list the number of athletes who have helped me fine-tune my coaching abilities; you know who you are. Between my highly talented athletes to those who struggled to advance, I became sharper and more skilled at helping others. I suppose every coach who works hard for long enough goes through the same thing. I took a lot of advice from established coaches back then too, such as Rich Lansky, Harvey Newton, and David Tullis from Lake Brantley High School. As my program grew, so did my need for assistant coaches. I couldn't be where I am today without the coaches who put in years of dedication with me: Amanda Cox, Josue Rodriguez, Stephen Adams, Robin Feuerman, Sara Campbell, and Samantha Tollman. They have all moved on in some capacity, some very recently, but remain in my network and a part of this book in some way. In their place are the assistant coaches I have now, Orlando Camargo Jr. (business partner), Amy Graham, Tracey Rife, and Justin Phillips, Jessica Rodriguez, Elizabeth Hautamaki, and Rachel Batista. They are my support and without them I couldn't wear the multiple hats that I do.

And so I end for the time being with this book, the idea for which came to me after mentoring so many future head coaches. I have been giving back what was given to me. It's about lineage! I felt what better way to continue to help others than by sharing information on identifying errors and providing cues and corrections for coaches and athletes. Writing always intimidated me but thanks to my athlete Melissa Baldwin, the process of documenting my thoughts turned out not to be such a nightmare. Her advice and editing helped shape the flow of this book. I thank Greg Everett with Catalyst Athletics for agreeing to publish my work and for having the faith in me to support it from its beginning.

Thank you all who have been in my weightlifting life, and who are with me now, including my wife Jill Farris, and our children, Isabella & Donovan Camargo, for putting up with my long nights and early days. I love you three so much for that.

For those not mentioned, you know who you are and you too have a piece of this book. Thank you.

CONTENTS

ERROR INDEX

SNATCH ERRORS

CLEAN ERRORS

JERK ERRORS

PROGRESSIONS

The number one priority when learning the Olympic weightlifting movements is controlling the path of the bar. Speed and explosiveness will come later down the line, but only when bar control has been achieved consistently.

There are numerous ways to teach someone new to Olympic weightlifting how to perform the snatch and clean & jerk. The optimum way to do so is with a step-by-step, simple-leading-into-complex method better known as *progressions*. Using an analogy made by the first assistant coach I ever had, Amanda Cox, it's a method of teaching A, followed by A+B, followed by A+B+C, and so forth, where each step taught includes the one before it.

The next few pages will describe my system of introducing the snatch, clean, and then jerk to someone for the first time. Included with these steps are the reasons why I've found them so effective and time-efficient.

It is recommended the athlete use a light barbell when possible rather than a PVC pipe or dowel. The slight resistance of a barbell makes it easier for the athlete to feel the positions. In all steps, the number of reps and sets performed by the athlete is solely at the discretion of the coach. There should be enough repetitions to show competency in the positions without fatiguing the athlete excessively.

SNATCH PROGRESSIONS

POWER POSITION

The power position is the most vital part of the Olympic weightlifting movements. To not have this position down efficiently is to be limited in maximal lifts. Having determined his or her grip, the athlete should stand straight with feet directly below the hips (Note: This foot position or stance may change once the athlete has become comfortable with the movement). Take note of where the bar lies rested against the body and encourage the athlete to leave it at that location as he or she is asked to progress into the next few steps. The athlete will then slightly bend the knees without moving any other part of the body. The athlete must be flat-footed with the majority of the weight distributed towards the heels. The arms should be straight, elbows out, shoulders directly above the bar or behind it, and pushing the knees out is recommended but not necessary.

Because the power position is so important, it is the first step in teaching. It is the only way to produce optimum velocity on the bar because it keeps the bar in close proximity to the hips and legs. Failing to perform this in the lift will more than likely mean the barbell is too far away from the body, causing a weaker performance.

Standing tall (left) versus the power position (right)

POWER POSITION HOP & LAND

The athlete is asked to hop in the air, without moving the upper body at all, and land flat on the feet. This is not to say that the athlete should be encouraged to hang for long in the air or to stomp the feet. The desired movement is a short hop and flat landing, almost feeling as if he or she is landing on the heels. This sensation may be odd to the beginner, but it will prove beneficial as it's perfected.

> This emphasizes how important leg drive is to the movement. Educate the athlete on the triple extension, and focus less on hips and more on legs. The lower body plays such a dominant role that encouraging jumping (at a controlled height) is a must. Also, landing flat on the feet as opposed to the toes will introduce the athlete to the stability needed when "catching" the bar in the coming segments.

Power position hop & land

POWER SNATCH (POWER POSITION)

The athlete will add to the hop in the previous step by pulling the barbell all the way into the overhead position. The key here is to cue the athlete to lock out the elbows at the same time the feet land flat. The athlete is to receive the weightless barbell in a quarter-depth squat. Once stabilization has occurred, the athlete may rise to a straight leg position. Keeping the barbell close to the body as it is pulled into the overhead position is vital in order to maintain control of its trajectory (path). The athlete may not bend the arms until the hop has been initiated.

> This will be the first time the athlete is introduced to the "catch." Performing this simple step correctly, without the complications of picking it up from the ground, will carry over as the athlete moves on to more complex positions of the snatch. Locking the elbows overhead simultaneously with the feet landing on the floor teaches the athlete the stability needed once heavy load is implemented. Any delay with this timing will delay the steadiness needed to hold heavy weight and thus put the athlete at risk of failure.

Power Snatch from the Power Position

POWER SNATCH (MID-HANG)

The athlete will now be taught for the first time how to bend over with the barbell while maintaining a neutral spine. This may pose a problem for many and it's important they perform this correctly before being allowed to progress to the next step. The barbell should be taken down to the mid-hang position, which is directly above the knee caps. Shoulders must be in front of the plane of the barbell and knees remain as bent as they were in the power position. Do not let the athlete bend the knees further as he or she would in a squat. The athlete should feel significant tension in the hamstrings. On command, the athlete will shift back into the power position, and without hesitation, perform the previous step (Power Snatch - Power Position). This is an important time to emphasize patience, control, and the necessity for the athlete to keep the bar close to the body.

> This particular hang position allows the athlete to understand that tension of the hamstrings is important and teaches them how to maintain a flat or even concave back while bent over. By teaching this mid-hang position, the coach can illustrate to the athlete how to pivot on the hips and teach the importance of velocity without adding too much complexity.

Power snatch (mid-hang)

POWER SNATCH (LOW-HANG)

Taking the hang position further, the athlete is now asked to lower the barbell to below the knee caps. There should be no more bending of the knees; they stay as bent as they were in the power position and the mid-hang position. It's only a closing of the hips. On command, the athlete will shift through the previous position (mid-hang) and into the power position, and without hesitation, extend into the power snatch (receiving position).

> Though the distance between this step and the previous (mid-hang) is normally only a couple of inches, the steps are distinct and must be separated due to the navigation of the knee caps. Steering past the knees can be troubling for some beginners. In order for the athlete to successfully track the bar, the knees must be pulled back (not straightened completely) while the bar passes them during a lift. This stage allows the athlete to learn that concept.

Power snatch (low-hang)

POWER SNATCH (FLOOR)

This will be the first time the athlete is exposed to the start position and lifting from the ground. This presents the most complex posture for the athlete. Though every frame is different, an ideal starting stance should have the feet directly under the hips, toes slightly turned out, knees flaring out (contact of the arms is permitted), arms straight, elbows facing outward, hook-grip utilized, shoulders slightly in front of the plane of the bar (as it has been since the mid-hang position), hips slightly higher than the height of the knees, back flat or extended, and eyes focused straight ahead. Once this posture is obtained, the athlete will be asked to elevate the bar, keeping this posture the exact same as they pass the low-hang position and mid-hang position, then shift the barbell into the hips to achieve the power position, and without hesitation, perform the power snatch (receive).

> This is near the final product, as it is the snatch from the ground, minus the squat portion (making it a power snatch), which is forthcoming. It's important that time is spent on effectively setting the ideal starting stance. Finding a comfortable start will expedite the learning process and the athlete may soon begin training regularly in the snatch. This is also the best opportunity to introduce the idea of picking up the barbell with control but immediately adding acceleration so that they enter the power position with maximum velocity.

Power snatch (floor)

POWER SNATCH + OVERHEAD SQUAT

In this stage the athlete is asked to perform the same movement as in the previous step (Power Snatch - Floor) but separately add an overhead squat. The overhead squat will expose possible limitations in the athlete's mobility.

> Special attention should be made to the athlete's flexibility and any deficiencies. Should there be problems in the shoulders, thoracic (upper) back, hips, or ankles that prevent him or her from performing a proper overhead squat, they should be addressed before or after training, as a warm-up or cool-down respectively. It's highly recommended that an athlete squat only so far as present mobility allows with proper form. The depth at which posture breaks down should be considered that

Power snatch + overhead squat

athlete's overhead squat maximum depth for the time being. Pushing them lower with improper posture may only cause harm. This can be a sensitive, challenging feat to perform. As such, this stage calls for the power snatch to be separate from the overhead squat.

THE SNATCH

The final step is to put it all together. The athlete will, in one motion, and without hesitation, lift the barbell from the floor into the overhead position and squat. Saying *snatch* automatically implies a full squat; other variations would be specified (e.g. power snatch).

A common cue that coaches use is "lift slowly until the knees, then go fast." I'm not a fan of this tactic because there is too drastic of a change when dealing with heavy loads, and encouraging slow movement, any time, will limit an athlete's force production. In the end, coaches using this cue are attempting to teach the athlete control. As such, use this "control" cue instead, as it will make the point without restricting power output. It's recommended the athlete learn how to lift off the floor with control, but immediately begin accelerating the bar to its maximum velocity, in the power position.

In the majority of cases, this final stage can be achieved in the first lesson for the beginner. Once attained, training can begin. The training to be prescribed is at the discretion of the coach. It is highly recommended that beginners not attempt maximal lifts just yet. They must show proficiency in the movement in order to perform it with heavy loads. In the rare cases that this final stage cannot be attained within the first lesson, it's advised the coach take the athlete to whichever position they were last able to perform correctly. There is nothing wrong with keeping an athlete at one of the above steps for several lessons until they show enough proficiency. If redundancy becomes a concern, the coach may easily introduce the athlete to other routines or exercises that will stimulate their interests.

The snatch

CLEAN PROGRESSIONS

POWER POSITION

As mentioned in the Snatch Progressions, the power position is the most vital part of the Olympic weightlifting movements. To not master this position is to be limited in your maximal lifts. Having determined the grip, athletes should stand straight with their feet directly below the hips (Note: This foot position or stance may change once an athlete has become comfortable with the movement). Take note of where the bar lies resting on the body, and encourage the athlete to leave it at that location as he or she is asked to progress into the next few steps. The location of the bar may be slightly lower than it is with the snatch grip. This should not cause any concern. In the end, so long as it's within the region between the top of the thighs and waistline, it's acceptable. The athlete will then slightly bend the knees without moving any other part of the body. The athlete must be flat-footed with the majority of the weight distributed towards the heels. Arms are straight, elbows out, shoulders directly above the bar or behind it, and pushing the knees out is recommended but not necessary.

> Because the power position is so important, it is the first step in teaching. It is the only way to produce optimum velocity on the bar because it keeps the bar in close proximity to the hips and legs. Performance will be greatly inhibited should the athlete fail to arrive at the power position.

Standing straight (left) versus power position (right)

POWER POSITION HOP & LAND

The athlete is asked to hop in the air, without moving the upper body at all, and land flat on the feet. This is not to say that the athlete should be encouraged to float for long in the air or to stomp the feet. The desired movement is a short hop and flat landing, almost feeling as if he or she is landing on the heels. This sensation may be odd to the beginner but it will prove beneficial as it is perfected.

> This emphasizes how important leg drive is to the movement. Educate the athlete on the triple extension, and focus less on hips and more on legs. The lower body plays such a dominant role that encouraging jumping (at a controlled height) is a must. Also, landing flat on the feet as opposed to the toes will introduce the athlete to the stability needed when "catching" the bar in the coming segments.

Power position hop & land

RECEIVING POSITION

Taking a brief break from dynamic movements, the athlete should be shown a proper rack position, with elbows up high, feet in a wider stance in preparation for a squat (to be introduced in later steps) and a slight bend of the knees. I often ask athletes to hold this position until the first signs of fatigue in order to teach body awareness. After the brief hold, the athlete will reset back into the power position.

> This "catching" position, much like for the snatch, must be introduced to the athlete as it will be the point where an athlete's functional stability is challenged most. That is, the barbell in a normal clean will become weightless for a brief moment, then travel downward. The body must be in a strong, stable position underneath it before it reaches the floor. Showing the athlete this step will allow him or her to recognize a structurally sound position; developing the strength will follow with time.

Rack position (left) and receiving position (right)

POWER CLEAN (POWER POSITION)

The athlete will add to the hop in the earlier step by pulling the barbell to the shoulders and landing in the receiving position he or she held in the previous step. The key here is to cue the athlete to shoot their elbows as high as possible at the same time their feet land flat. The athlete is to receive the weightless barbell in a quarter-depth squat. Once stabilization has occurred, he or she may rise to a straight leg position. Keeping the barbell close to the body as it is pulled to the shoulders is vital in order to maintain control of its trajectory (path). The athlete may not bend the arms until the hop has been initiated.

This will be the first time the athlete is introduced to the "catch" in full speed. Performing this simple step correctly, without the complications of picking it up from the ground, will carry over as the athlete moves on to more complex positions of the clean. Quick elbows as high as possible, with the barbell in full contact from shoulder to shoulder, simultaneously with the feet landing on the floor teaches the athlete the stability needed once heavy load is implemented. Any delay with this timing will delay the steadiness needed to hold heavy weight and thus put the athlete at risk of failure.

Power clean (power position)

POWER CLEAN (MID-HANG)

The athlete will now be introduced to bending over with the barbell while maintaining a neutral spine. This may pose a problem for many and it's important they perform this correctly before being allowed to progress to the next step. The barbell should be taken down to the mid-hang position, which is directly above the knee caps. Shoulders must be in front of the plane of the barbell and knees remain as bent as they were in the power position. Do not let the athlete bend the knees further as he or she would in a squat. The athlete should feel significant tension in the hamstrings. On command, the athlete will shift back into the power position, and without hesitation, perform the previous step (power clean - power position). This is an important time to emphasize patience, control, and the necessity for the athlete to keep the bar close to the body.

> This particular hang position allows the athlete to understand that tension of the hamstrings is important and teaches them how to maintain a flat or even concave back while bent over. By teaching this mid-hang position, the coach can illustrate to the athlete how to pivot on the hips, and teach the importance of velocity without adding too much complexity.

Power clean (mid-hang)

POWER CLEAN (LOW-HANG)

Taking the hang position further, the athlete is now asked to lower the barbell to below the kneecaps. There should be no more bending of the knees; they stay as bent as they were in the power position and the mid-hang position. It's only a matter of closing the hips. On command, the athlete will shift through the previous position (mid-hang) and into the power position and, without hesitation, extend into the power clean receiving position.

> Though the distance between this step and the previous (mid-hang) is normally only a couple of inches, the steps are distinct and must be separated, due to the navigation of the kneecaps. Steering past the knees can be troubling for some beginners. In order for the athlete to successfully track the bar, the knees must be pulled back (not straightened completely) while the bar passes them during a lift. This stage allows the athlete to learn that concept.

Power clean (low-hang)

POWER CLEAN (FLOOR)

This will be the first time the athlete is exposed to the start position: lifting from the ground. This presents the most complex posture for the athlete. Though every frame is different, an ideal starting stance should have the feet directly under the hips, toes slightly turned out, knees flaring out (contact of the arms is permitted), arms straight, elbows facing outward, hook-grip utilized, shoulders slightly in front of the plane of the bar (as they have been since the mid-hang position), hips slightly higher than the height of the knees, back flat or extended, and eyes focused straight ahead. Once this posture is obtained, the athlete will be asked to elevate the bar, keeping this posture the exact same as they pass the low-hang position and mid-hang position, then shift the barbell into the hips to satisfy the power position, and without hesitation, perform the power clean (receive).

> This is near the final product as it is the clean from the ground, minus the squat portion (making it a power clean), which is forthcoming. It's important that time is spent on effectively setting the ideal starting stance. Finding a comfortable start will expedite the learning process and the athlete may soon begin training regularly in the clean. This is also the best opportunity to introduce the idea of picking up the barbell with control but immediately adding acceleration so that the athlete enters the power position with maximum velocity.

Power clean (floor)

POWER CLEAN + FRONT SQUAT

In this stage the athlete is asked to perform the same movement as in the previous step (power clean - floor) but separately add a front squat. The front squat will expose possible limitations in the athlete's mobility.

> Special attention should be paid to the athlete's flexibility and any deficiencies. Should there be problems with flexibility in the shoulders, hips, or ankles that prevent the athlete from performing a proper front squat, they should be addressed accordingly with stretching or foam rolling prior to or after training, as a warm-up or cool-down respectively. It's highly recommended that an athlete squat only so far as present mobility allows using proper form. The depth at which posture breaks down should be considered that athlete's maximal front squat depth for the time being. Pushing the athlete low-

Power clean + front squat

er with improper posture may only cause harm. This can be a sensitive, challenging feat to perform. As such, this stage calls for the power clean to be performed separately from the front squat.

THE CLEAN

The final product is to put it all together. From the floor the athlete will, in one motion and without hesitation, lift the barbell into the receiving position and squat. To say "clean" automatically implies a full squat. Other variations would be specified (e.g. power clean).

The clean

A common cue that coaches use is "lift slowly until the knees, then go fast." I'm not a fan of this tactic because there is too drastic of a change when dealing with heavy loads, and encouraging slow movement, any time, will limit an athlete's force production. In the end, coaches using this cue are attempting to teach the athlete control. As such, use this "control" cue instead, as it will make the point without restricting power output. It's recommended the athlete learn how to lift off the floor with control, and then gradually accelerate the bar to its maximum velocity, in power position.

> In the majority of cases, this final stage can be achieved in the first lesson for the beginner. Once attained, training can begin. The training to be prescribed is at the discretion of the coach. It is highly recommended that beginners not attempt maximal lifts just yet. They must show proficiency in the movement in order to perform it with heavy loads. In the rare cases that this final stage cannot be attained within the first lesson, it's advised the coach take the athlete to whichever position he or she was last able to perform correctly. There is nothing wrong with keeping an athlete at one of the above steps for several lessons until they show enough proficiency. If redundancy becomes a concern, the coach may easily introduce the athlete to other routines or exercises that will stimulate their interest.

JERK PROGRESSIONS

FOOT STANCE

By definition, any type of a jerk (power, push, split, or squat) means a dip, drive, and a re-dip or "catch." In this book, I'll focus on the split jerk, as all the other types need far less introduction, including the squat jerk. As such, the word *jerk* will automatically refer to the split jerk. Since the split jerk causes people so much trouble, it's best to start with foot stance. Which foot should the athlete place forward? There are several ways of determining this, including the push method (stand behind the athlete and give a light shove to see which leg they brace themselves with), the drop method (same concept but the coach will have the athlete lean on the coach's extended arm and let go, allowing the athlete to again brace themselves) or by simply asking the athlete which leg is their "dominant" leg. I've used them all. The idea is that the athlete will automatically place in front whichever leg feels most natural. However, after the first several years of coaching I felt these tactics still left too much room for error. So, I began to use the Sprinter's Position method and have used it exclusively. I have not used any other method for ten years now. It's very simple to apply to beginners.

Ask them to stand as they would if engaged in a full-out sprint. In the end, how they pose is of no concern to the coach; it only determines which leg to place forward in the jerk. Will it stay that way? Not necessarily. It's a starting point. Hopefully the coach secures the correct stance and there is never a switch. However, no matter how good the coach is, there exists a small percentage of athletes who, after being shown the split for the first time, later switch feet. There's no guaranteed formula. That said, I feel the Sprinter's Position is the most accurate and I've found there is less occurrence of switching the feet later.

Using sprinter's position to determine split stance

Because the sprinter's position is something we all develop as children, it comes far more naturally than any other foot-determining method above. So long as the athlete is unaware of the reason why you're asking them to display a sprinter's stance, the result should be the position in which they feel most powerful. If the coach hints at his or her intention, or if it is explained ahead of time, then the athlete is likely to over think it and the accuracy could be jeopardized.

FOOT PLACEMENT & RECOVERY

From here, the coach will then place the legs in the desired positions: Front shin vertical, back leg bent with heel off the ground, and torso vertical. We must remember that we have two legs, and they both should bear the weight of the lifter and the barbell. I do not believe in distributing more weight on the front leg than the rear. I prefer even distribution where both legs have 50% of the total weight. Once the desired position has been met, ask the athlete to hold in it until the first signs of fatigue in order to teach body awareness. After the brief hold, the athlete will reset back into the start stance by taking a step back with the front leg and following with a

Foot placement and recovery

forward step of the rear leg (a two-step process). The steps should return the athlete to where he or she began, which is the same stance taken from the floor during a clean.

> Understanding proper foot placement is a must, but recovering with controlled steps will either make or break the lift. It's the completion of the jerk process. Leading with the front leg tends to provide more control for the athlete. Though athletes can feel stable relying heavily on the front leg and leading with the rear leg, this tends to cause athletes to step forward. This moves the barbell forward and puts the athlete at risk of taking excessive measures to recover back to the beginning stance.

FOOT SPLITTING

Once the stance and recovery method has been established it's a great idea to have the athlete practice the process of moving the feet into the split position at full speed. The number of reps and sets performed by the athlete is solely at the discretion of the coach. There should be enough repetitions to show competency in the positions without fatiguing the athlete excessively.

Foot splitting

This drill, referred to USA Weightlifting as "Foot Work Drill", gives the athlete consistency. Once weight is introduced, the athlete will find it more difficult, so having him or her get used to the switching of foot stance at full speed develops confidence and better prepares the athlete for the ultimate goal of maximum weight.

THE JERK

The final product is the jerk. Here the barbell is introduced for the first time. With it touching the shoulders, the athlete is asked to dip and drive the bar into the overhead position. The catch portion will be in the split

The jerk

stance described above. The athlete should be asked to hold the split once again with the bar overhead for a few seconds. Once control has been established, the athlete may recover as described above, keeping the bar overhead until the feet are aligned with each other. Then, the bar may be lowered.

> By asking the athlete to hold the weight overhead in the split stance, the coach can determine if the athlete can show balance. This will also allow the athlete to have better body awareness, and shifting or loss of balance will be exposed at this point. The position can be critiqued and then adjusted for the next repetition. This is the proper time to promote safety and instruct the athlete not to lower the barbell until his or her feet are realigned. Lowering it any sooner puts them at risk of losing balance, and with heavy load, could cause injury.

FINAL RACK POSITION

Unlike the progressions of the snatch or clean, the final step in learning the jerk isn't performing it as described in the last step. The last thing to be addressed is actually the shoulder set up. Here the athlete is given the distinction between the rack position of the clean versus the rack position for the jerk. In the clean, it is highly advantageous for the athlete to keep elbows as high as possible. Letting the barbell rest only on the fingertips is permissible. However, prior to the jerk, it's best to lower the elbows to prepare for the straight-arm lock out. Since the end position is overhead with straight arms, we must accommodate that by placing the elbows downward. To have the elbows up high will only increase the time it takes to straighten the arms. How far down? As far as possible without compromising the security of the barbell on the shoulders. Should the coach see the bar slide down or move from a secure place, then the elbows have gone too far and should be raised a bit more. Lastly, flaring the elbows out allows for a flatter thoracic (upper) back. This flattening provides a stronger base of support. In contrast, having elbows facing inward causes a convex, rounded upper back, which is a weaker posture. Once the proper posture in the pre-jerk is established, the athlete should then return to practice the jerk.

> The athlete will benefit from a stronger, more structurally-sound rack position if the elbows can drop a bit and flare outward. This opens up the chest cavity and actually makes breathing easier than high elbows that are facing inward. Moreover, the ability to take a large amount of air immediately before the execution of the jerk maximizes strength. This proper set up for the jerk will also shorten the time it takes to receive the bar in the overhead position, which for many is invaluable.

Clean rack position (left) versus jerk rack position (right)

CUES & CORRECTIONS

It must be noted that anyone with some level of competency can show another how to perform a snatch, clean, and jerk. What separates coaches is the ability to correct individual errors. I'll take that a step further by saying what separates elite coaches is their ability to train someone over a long period of time while maintaining forward progress. No matter the level of experience, practitioners of Olympic weightlifting will always work on their form. Ask elite lifters, and they'll tell you that even at their level they still find ways to perfect their technique. That's not to say they are struggling with their form by any means. Those days have long passed. They are extremely proficient and consistent. It's a matter of tweaking, changing, and, in some cases, returning to a tactic they employ, in order to gain the advantage over their competition.

So it follows, corrections are key in that they must be applied, to varying degrees, to all we instruct. It can be easy to spot when a correction must be made, but errors are not always so easy to fix and some have multiple causes. To say an athlete is "jumping forward" during a snatch is great, but quite obvious and incomplete. Why are they? Can the coach identify at specifically what point during the lift the error occurs and make the proper correction? That ability is what separates advanced coaches from new trainers.

Cues: we love to find great ones. Cues are words or expressions that elicit a desired physical response from the athlete. Not all cues are literal. In fact, many are figurative. I'm proud of the cues I carry in my arsenal. They come from two unique places: directly from the mouths of athletes, and years of accumulation. My vocabulary of cues took quite some time to develop and they often times come right out automatically. Over the years, when an athlete has completed a lift I have asked him or her to describe what it felt like, whether good or bad. I, in turn, use the same words they speak when coaching them. For example, a lifter successfully corrects an error in the snatch and says he felt the bar was "snapped behind my ears." I'll then use "snap behind the ears" as much as necessary on that one athlete to remind him how to make the bar land. I'll perhaps use the same cue on others to see if they too respond the same way.

The biggest mistake a coach can make is over-coaching, or over-cueing. Too many instructions will cause confusion and in turn slow the learning process down. This section describes the most common errors and my suggested corrections and cues. This is hardly an exhaustive list, but rather, and, perhaps more significantly, contains the successful cues I have accumulated in my years of experience.

Some things to think about:

> Video recording and reviewing an athlete's technique is beneficial, especially in slower motion or frame by frame. However, be careful not to use video to the extent where the athlete suffers from "analysis paralysis." Too much exposure to video footage can cause athletes to over think.
>
> Never use mirrors. The use of mirrors will only slow athletes down. By the time their minds compute what their eyes see, and attempt to send signals to their bodies, the lift should be over. There may be no harm in moving slowly in front of a mirror with a PVC pipe or dowel rod. However, training in front of one during high speed, high intensity attempts, will only ruin the movement they may have otherwise perfected.
>
> Many drills, which are described later in this book, serve dual purposes.
>
> The goal is to feel the movement, not to see it or think it.

SNATCH CUES & CORRECTIONS

The snatch, though seemingly complex, is actually simple to conceptualize. There are far fewer moving parts than the clean & jerk. What intimidates people about the snatch is the amount of balance and mobility needed to be highly successful. Moreover, there is a smaller margin of error in this lift versus any other associated with Olympic weightlifting. The snatch is far more about precision, whereas the clean & jerk is more about effort. An athlete can commit more errors in the clean & jerk and still walk away successful compared to the snatch, making it my favorite of the three lifts.

JUMPING FORWARD

This is a big concern, and simply telling the athlete he or she is jumping forward isn't enough. Determining exactly where (or in which phase of the lift) the problem originates is essential. There are three factors, or a combination of any of them, which cause an athlete to jump forward: being forward on the first first pull, early on the toes during the transition, or swinging the bar out during the second pull.

Causes
Athletes jump forward because it feels explosive to them. We are all more agile and explosive on the balls of our feet, so we try to rely on them wherever possible, even at the detriment of proper bar path.

FORWARD OFF THE FLOOR (FIRST PULL FORWARD)

Cues

- "Chest up"
- "Heels into floor" (this is not to mean lean back; keep the athlete in place but have them drive the heels into the floor)
- "Knees out"
- "Move hips and bar together"
- "Sweep back"

Corrections

- Lift-Offs (practicing keeping the knees back and out of the way)
- Snatch Grip Deadlifts (practicing the hips and bar rising at the same rate)
- Any exercise that will keep the athlete flat on the feet immediately pulling off the floor will be advantageous

EARLY TOES PAST THE KNEES

Cues

- "Stay on heels"
- "Delay the jump"
- "Patience"
- "Wait on the bar"
- "No rush"
- "Get knees back under the bar"

Corrections

- Mid-hang high pulls
- Mid-hang snatch
- Power position snatch
- Any snatch from technique blocks that rests the bar at knee height

Coach's Tip: As in the first pull, people want to increase velocity so the natural thing to do is shift to the toes, as we are all more powerful and agile there. However, for beginners and intermediate athletes this can cause the barbell to travel too far forward when we want them to maintain more weight distribution on their heels. Athletes should perform any exercise that will instill patience and keep them flat-footed a bit longer during this phase of the lift.

SENDING BAR OUT AND AWAY FROM THE BODY IN SECOND PULL

Cues

- "Keep bar close"
- "Jump and high-pull the bar"
- "Aim for the chin"

- "Jump from the heels"
- Describe how they should imagine the bar is so close it will pull their shirt off

Corrections

- Dip snatch
- Snatch high-pull + snatch
- Any snatch variation that does not include a hang (as this may reinforce the problem), keeping the bar moving up and back to the end position.

Coach's Tip: Athletes love the feeling of striking the barbell with the hips. It does provide great propulsion. However, bar path is compromised. The bar must always stay directly above the area of the feet from start to finish. Therefore, the bar must be jumped vertically, not forward.

EARLY ARM BEND

Is bending the arms too early a real problem? Not in all cases. Early arm bending is only bad if the athlete, during the second pull, straightens the arms out and re-bends a second time. This will certainly cause a loss of tension, which can reduce the speed of the bar. The athlete who bends the arms early but keeps the arms bent, maintaining tension, can probably get away with it! If, however, the early arm bend is problematic, below are the fixes.

Causes

Athletes commit this error because they are either trying to create the very thing the power position is supposed to do for them, which is velocity, or attempting to strike the barbell against the hips.

Cues

- "Long arms"
- "Straight arms"
- "Let the arms hang"

Corrections

- Power position snatch
- Power position high-pulls
- Power position shrugs
- Adjust grip so that the bar enters higher into the hips as they enter the second pull since many times people bend their arms early in an attempt to "hit the right spot." However, be cautious not to negatively effect their overhead position. The priority in the snatch is comfort overhead. As such, adjustment of the grip just to accommodate hip contact of the power position should be done carefully.

Coach's Tip: Believe it or not, the best way to fix early arm bend is to not focus on the arms at all, but rather the power position. Many people bend their arms early because they're trying to create the very thing the power position is supposed to do for them—velocity.

FAILING TO DROP UNDER THE BAR (ABLE-BODIED)

Do you or someone you coach refuse to drop under the bar in the snatch? Or do you or your athlete drop under the bar with light weight but not once it gets heavy? Failing to drop under the bar is common and an indication that an athlete isn't comfortable yet being low under the bar. There are flexibility issues to consider, and if an athlete suffers from significant mobility issues, they must conquer those restrictions first. (Even in a power snatch, there should be some degree of depth under the bar in order to lift more weight.) So, for those who can, but won't, here's how to get them there.

Causes

This happens because the athlete isn't comfortable yet being low under the bar, mainly because their squatting ability is underdeveloped. Mobility in the shoulders, hips, and/or ankles is also a large factor.

Cues

- "Commit"
- "Dive under"
- "Don't be shy"
- "Pull and Under"
- "Lock and land" (indicating the elbows should lock out overhead at the same time the feet land)

Corrections

- Power snatch + overhead squat
- Pause overhead
- Dip snatch
- Tall snatch
- Snatch balance
- Drop snatch
- Sots press (aka snatch press from squat position)
- Flexibility exercises that will improve mobility and ability to squat under the bar in an overhead squat position
- Any exercise that will get rid of the fear of being under the bar
- Explain to the athlete that a great pull is no good if it is not coupled with a drop under. It's a two-part equation. One cannot live without the other and in fact, to be more proficient in one without the equal ability to perform the other, will lead to failure.
- Power snatching only will greatly limit the athlete.

HIPS RISING FASTER THAN THE BAR OR SHOULDERS (AKA STRIPPER PULL)

In order to set up the transition into power position, then second pull, the athlete needs to keep the hips rising at the same rate as the bar immediately off the floor. It's the same thing as saying the hips should move at the same rate as the shoulders. Failure to accomplish this will slow the speed of the bar or ruin the timing of the mechanics needed past the knees and into to the hips. Here are some suggestions.

Causes

The athlete creates this error to get a sense of speed off the floor but it is an illusion. What they're actually doing is moving their bodies fast without the bar reacting with it. Be careful, however, this doesn't mean coaches should promote a slow first pull.

Cues

- "Hips down"
- "Chest up"
- "Hips and bar"
- "Hips and shoulders"
- "Arch the back"
- "Keep the chest rising"

Corrections

- Lift-offs
- Snatch halting deadlifts
- Any exercises that keep the hips and bar (or shoulders) moving at the same rate

Coach's Tip: Believe it or not, an athlete can get away with this error and "stripper pull" if they're able to raise the chest as well. This error becomes a problem only if the chest sinks while the hips rise. If the athlete can keep the chest up, then the quickly rising hips may not be an issue.

LOSING BAR BEHIND

If an athlete must lose the bar, then I would much rather he or she lose the bar behind them than in front. Why? It's an indicator they have enough power and direction to get the bar in the overhead squat position, as opposed to jumping forward or not having enough power.

Causes
Athletes commit this error for one simple reason: lack of control.

Cues

- "Vertical pull"
- "Sweet spot" (the spot where it's most comfortable for the athlete to receive the bar overhead)

Corrections

- High-hang snatch
- Dip snatch
- Power position snatch
- Tall snatch

Coach's Tip: Notice the corrections include a jump (extension) and catch. Bar control is priority number one when learning Olympic weightlifting. It's great to have explosive hips and to have speed, but it does no good if the athlete cannot control where the bar ends up. Triple-extending (opening/extension of ankles, knees and hips) during the second pull is the best way to keep control of the bar. Overextending the hips, or smacking the bar out and away from the body, will put the athlete at risk of losing control, or in the case of the snatch, looping the bar path behind the head.

MISSING POWER POSITION

There's no arguing that the power position is one of the most essential parts of Olympic weightlifting. In fact, it's the primary point I focus on when teaching. Power position ensures the bar stays close to the body, giving us more control, and allows us to optimize our power output. It's not easy for some people to produce at first.

Causes

Athletes miss the power position because they're relying on their arms more than their legs. It's more intuitive to use our arms to lift the bar but what's more effective is the use of the hips and legs.

Cues

- "Keep close"
- "Get into the hips"
- "Less arms, more legs"
- "Scoop" (an oldie but goodie)

Corrections

- Power position snatch
- Dip snatch
- Mid-hang snatch pulls
- Snatch high-pulls

Coach's Tip: More than likely the athlete is relying on the arms more than the legs. Our arms are not as strong as our legs. Given that, I am a huge advocate for the triple extension. We must give the athletes exercises that allow them to focus more on the hips and legs, not the arms. Also, remind the athlete not to "smack" the hips into the bar, unless they "smack" the bar vertically. I agree hip contact of the bar is beneficial so long as it can be directed in the proper way; which is not out and around the body. Some athletes successfully graze the upper legs and hips with the barbell without violently impacting the bar.

LANDING ON TOES INSTEAD OF FLAT-FOOTED

On Earth, what goes up must come down. The barbell is no different. When we jump the bar vertically, it will make its way down—and when it does, athletes need to have solid ground beneath them. First, let's address the width of the foot stance. I believe the pulling stance should be different than the squatting stance. The pulling stance should be narrow to allow the greatest verticality, whereas a wider stance will accommodate a comfortable squat. Next, landing flat on the feet is crucial. Striking with the toes first causes a slight delay, as it forces the athlete to then roll their feet onto the heels.

Causes

Athletes may land on their toes because it feels stronger to do so. As mentioned several times in this book, we all feel more agile and explosive on the balls of the feet. Relying on them more than heels feels more natural but it is not as effective.

Cues

- "Land flat"
- "Let me hear your feet land"

Corrections

- Snatch balance
- Drop snatch
- Foot work drills (no barbell, stand then drop into a squat)

Coach's Tip: When the athlete lands flat-footed, there will be a solid sound of the shoes. It should be noted that coaches want to avoid any excessive hang time. The goal is to have a swift shift of the feet, or the very least, solid strike of the shoes with minimal distance to the floor.

FAILURE TO TRIPLE EXTEND

Failing to triple-extend (straightening the ankles, knees, and hips) is often associated with having "muted" hips or not opening the hips all the way. Trainers often overemphasize the hips during the snatch, but the issue goes far beyond that. Hips are important, yes. However, overextending the hips may cause the bar to lose proper path. It's less about the hips and more about leg drive. It is feasible to "open" hips vertically, not just forward. Therefore, to fully extend the legs means to open the ankles, knees, and hips vertically. If you're visualizing this correctly, you got it, it's a jump. Unlike a jump, though, the aim is not to leave the ground excessively. The goal, rather, is to extend enough to propel the bar and move the feet in preparation for the squat. (If the athlete chooses not to squat, then he or she should at least land flat-footed.)

Causes

Athletes tend to rush the jump because the most dramatic phase of the lift is the catch. Athletes committing this error are focused on that very aspect and not first giving the lift time to develop.

Cues

- "Extend"
- "Finish"
- "Big pull"
- "Stay tall"
- "Jump longer"
- "Drop under at the last second"
- "Long legs"
- "Leg drive"

Corrections

- Tall snatch
- Snatch high-pull
- Snatch high-pull + snatch

Coach's Tip: The goal is to get the athlete to fully extend the legs and not shorten the jump cycle. They may be rushing to sneak under the bar. Yes, there is a risk they'll spend too much time leaving the ground with their feet. Should that occur, refer to the "Landing on toes" correction above. In the end, we don't want to create the famous "donkey kick" which causes the athlete to waste time in the air.

DONKEY KICK

In the act of becoming explosive, and being aggressive when receiving the barbell, athletes may develop the famous "Donkey Kick." This is when the athlete kicks the feet back while dropping under the barbell to receive it in an overhead position. This is a waste of valuable time and will delay the speed at which the athlete enters the squat with the barbell in the overhead position.

Causes

Athletes commit this error for no other reason but to feel explosive in the catch and to hear the loud sound of their feet when receiving the barbell.

Cues

- "Quick feet"
- "Drop under at the last second"
- "Stay taller longer" (this will force them under with less time to waste)

Corrections

- Tall snatch
- Drop snatch (not snatch balance as this may reinforce the problem)
- Snatch from technique blocks at high-hang or waist height.
- Foot work drills (no barbell, weightless, the athlete stands then drops into a squat)

Coach's Tip: The goal is for the athlete to be able to extend and propel the bar (moving the feet if they choose) but land flat-footed with minimal waste of time. Most athletes develop this error because they like the sound of their shoes striking the ground or enjoy the feeling of a violent "catch" of the barbell in the receiving position. Remind them it's possible to create the sound with the feet leaving the ground no more than a quarter of an inch.

THROWING HEAD BACK

Throwing the head back during the snatch can ruin technique for some athletes. Yes, it's possible to do so effectively and there are a few elite lifters who get away with it. It works for them and there's little argument against them using this tactic. However, for most others, throwing the head back leads to the bar looping out and around the body instead of remaining close and vertical. It may also lead to an imbalance in the receiving phase of the lift. Some shifting back of the head is permissible. It's the excessive whipping back that should raise concern for coaches.

Causes

Athletes commit this error to feel more powerful in the jump. It can be a bad habit for many, as the dramatic rotation of the head does nothing for true bar elevation.

Cues

- "Keep head straight"
- "Focus eyes in front"
- "Stare at the (chose an object in front of lifter)"

Corrections

- Tall snatch
- Establish focal point
- Any pulling movement while focusing on maintaining a neutral head. A little pull back is okay.

Coach's Tip: Vision plays a significant role in balance. Many athletes who throw their heads back tend to close their eyes and re-open them when they receive the barbell (without even realizing it), thereby compromising their balance. Ask them to choose a location in front of them, relatively high, that they can focus on during the entirety of the lift—perhaps something with lettering. Require them to read it during the lift. Beware the first time they fix the error they may report that they feel as if they did not have a "big pull", when in fact they did. Throwing one's head back does absolutely nothing for bar elevation. The athletes have merely developed the bad habit associating an explosive pull with the whipping motion of their heads.

KNEES IN THE WAY

Many new athletes do a fine job of shifting their knees back out of the way of the path of the bar when lifting off the ground without ever being told to. In the instances where an athlete doesn't do it automatically and instead tracks the barbell around his or her knees, the coach should address it accordingly. This error causes the athlete to slow the speed of the bar when it should be accelerating.

Causes

Athletes committing this error actually don't know they're doing it. It comes down to body awareness—they may not know that it's possible to move the knees out of the way and still be successful with the lift. It must be shown to them like any other introduction of a new exercise.

Cues

- "Knees back"
- "Drive heels into the floor"
- "Knees out"
- "No toes"
- "Start on heels and stay on them throughout the lift"
- "Sweep back"

Corrections

- Snatch-grip lift-off
- Snatch pull
- Low-hang snatch
- Halting snatch deadlifts at knee height
- Any pulling movement, moderately heavy, where the athlete can focus on the lift from the floor to the knees

Coach's Tip: Identifying the bar tracking around the knees is an easy observation to make. Like all corrections, however, fixing it is the challenging part. This error goes back to the topic of control, mentioned earlier in the *Hips rising faster than the bar or shoulders* error. Control from the floor is extremely important. Individuals with proportionately longer legs may suffer from this error more often. This error is one of the main reasons I prefer the start position to include hips slightly higher than the height of the knees. Please refer to the Snatch Progressions section of this book for the full list of a proper set up.

CLEAN CUES & CORRECTIONS

Many errors common to the snatch are also performed in the clean. The clean is the simplest of the three Olympic weightlifting movements, in my opinion. What does that say about the snatch and clean? They're execution is the same. The end location of the barbell is essentially the only difference. That said, there are a few differences between it and the snatch that will be covered in this section.

JUMPING FORWARD

This is a big concern and simply telling the athlete that he or she is jumping forward isn't enough. Determining exactly where (or in which phase of the lift) the problem originates is essential. There are three factors, or a combination of them, which cause an athlete to jump forward: being forward in the first pull, being on the toes early during the transition, or swinging the bar out during the second pull.

Causes

Athletes jump forward because it feels explosive to them. We are all more agile and explosive on the balls of our feet so we try and rely on them whenever possible, even at the detriment of proper bar path. The same can be said of striking the barbell with the hips. Though it provides great propulsion, bar path is compromised. The bar must always stay directly above the area of the feet from start to finish. Therefore, the bar must be jumped vertically, not outwardly.

FORWARD OFF THE FLOOR (FIRST PULL FORWARD)

Cues

- "Chest up"
- "Heels into floor" (this is not to mean lean back; keep the athlete in place but have them drive the heels into the floor)

- “Knees out”
- “Move hips and bar together”
- “Sweep back”

Corrections

- Clean lift-off (practicing keeping the knees back and out of the way)
- Clean-grip deadlift (practicing keeping the hips and bar rising at the same rate)
- Any exercise that will keep the athlete flat on the feet immediately off the floor will be advantageous.

EARLY ON THE TOES PAST THE KNEES

Cues

- “Stay on heels”
- “Delay the jump”
- “Patience”
- “Wait on the bar”
- “No rush”
- “Get knees back under the bar”

Corrections

- Mid-hang high-pull
- Mid-hang clean
- Power position clean
- Any clean from technique blocks that starts the bar at knee height

SENDING BAR OUT AND AWAY FROM THE BODY IN SECOND PULL

Cues

- “Keep bar close”
- “Elbows high”
- “Jump and high-pull the bar”
- “Jump from the heels”
- Describe how they should imagine the bar is so close it will pull their shirts off

Corrections

- Dip clean
- Clean high-pull + clean complex
- Any variation of the clean that does not include a hang (as this may reinforce the problem), keeping the bar moving up and back to the end position

FLIPPING THE BAR INTO THE RACK (AKA REVERSE-CURLING THE BAR)

This can be one of the most common errors when an athlete learns how to turn over the barbell into the rack position. Though it may seem more natural, it is an error that needs to be addressed because it will slow the rate at which the athlete can "catch" the bar. This error can also cause a crashing of the barbell onto the shoulders. Please also see *Crashing the bar* section below.

Causes

This error occurs for one of two reasons: the false sense of speed of the catch, or a lack of mobility (primarily internal rotation) preventing athletes from keeping their elbows high above the barbell during the pull. The barbell must travel in a path from the start to finish that is inches away from the body. This includes up the torso, following the chest, onto the shoulders in the rack position. To commit the error of flipping the barbell violates the proper bar path and delays the receiving phase of the lift. It will also make the bar feel heavier to the athlete.

Cues

- "High-pull the turnover"
- "Quick elbows"
- "Elbows stay above bar"

- "Scarecrow position"

Corrections
- Tall cleans
- Clean high-pull
- Clean high-pull + clean
- Upright row
- Clean turnover

EARLY ARM BEND

This error happens more frequently during the clean than the snatch, although some athletes commit it during both. Is bending the arms too early a real problem? Not in all cases. Early arm bending is only bad if the athlete, during the second pull, straightens the arms out and re-bends a second time. This will certainly cause a loss of tension, which can reduce the speed of the bar. The athlete who bends the arms early but keeps the arms bent, maintaining tension, can probably get away with it! If, however, the early arm bend is problematic, below are the fixes.

Causes
Athletes commit this error because they are either trying to create the very thing the power position is supposed to do for them, which is velocity, or attempting to strike the barbell into the hips in the exact location they do in the snatch. For this reason, arm bending can be more often seen in the clean than in the snatch. The best way to fix early arm bend is not to focus on the arms at all, but rather on the power position. The athlete will be successful as long as the bar makes contact in the region between the top of the quadriceps and the waistline, which encompasses the large, powerful muscle groups of the hip flexors, glutes, and legs.

Cues

- "Long arms"
- "Straight arms"
- "Let the arms hang"

Corrections

- Power position clean
- Power position clean high-pull
- Adjust the grip so that the bar enters higher into the hips as they enter the second pull since many times people bend their arms early in an attempt to "hit the right spot." However, be cautious of this as the rack position cannot be compromised. The rack position needs to remain as comfortable as possible for the athlete. Adjusting the grip only to accommodate hip contact could prove detrimental if not done carefully.

FAILING TO DROP UNDER THE BAR (ABLE-BODIED)

Failing to drop under the bar into a squat, when an athlete is fully capable of doing so, is a common error among beginners. A great pull is no good if it is not coupled with a drop under—it's a two-part equation. One cannot live without the other, and, in fact, to be more proficient in one without the equal ability to perform the other, will lead to failure. (Even in a power clean, there should be some degree of depth under the bar in order to lift more weight.) If an athlete suffers from significant mobility issues, however, they must conquer those restrictions first.

Causes

This happens because the athlete isn't comfortable yet being low under the bar, mainly because their squatting ability is underdeveloped. An athlete may declare they're better at the power clean than the clean. We all are when we begin. The squat must be trained, and therefore patience must be instilled in the athlete as they learn. Power cleaning only will greatly limit the athlete in the long term.

Cues

- "Commit"
- "Dive under"
- "Do not be shy"
- "Pull and Under"
- "Elbows and feet" (indicating their elbows should be through the bar in the rack position at the same time their feet land)

Corrections

- Squats, squats, and more squats of any kind, preferably front squats
- Dip clean
- Tall clean
- Flexibility exercises that will improve mobility and ability to squat under the bar in the rack position

HIPS RISING FASTER THAN THE BAR OR SHOULDERS (AKA STRIPPER PULL)

In order to set up the transition into power position, then second pull, the athlete needs to keep the hips rising at the same rate as the bar immediately off the floor. It's the same thing as saying the hips should move at the same rate as the shoulders. Failure to accomplish this will slow the speed of the bar or ruin the timing of the mechanics needed past the knees and into the hips.

Causes

The athlete creates this error to get a sense of speed off the floor, but it is an illusion. What the athlete is actually doing is moving the body rapidly, but failing to advance the bar in conjunction. Be careful, however, this doesn't mean coaches should promote a slow first pull. While I understand the intent behind the trainer's cue of "slow off the floor," I am strongly against using that cue. If coaches continuously cue their athletes to pull slowly off the floor, it's exactly what they'll do on a maximal lift, and slow is not what we want. Instead, the athlete must be taught control. What is control? Fixing this error and being able to lift from the floor with the hips and shoulders moving at the same rate. Theoretically, athletes can initiate a lift at full speed so long as they are controlled. Encourage a solid pick-up followed by a steady, continuous acceleration into the jump. Furthermore, believe it or not, athletes can get away with this error and "stripper-pull" if they're able to raise the chest as well. This error becomes a problem only if the chest sinks while the hips rise. If an athlete can keep the chest up, then the quickly rising hips may not be an issue.

Cues

- "Hips down"
- "Chest up"
- "Hips and bar"
- "Hips and shoulders"
- "Arch the back"
- "Keep the chest rising"

Corrections

- Clean lift-off
- Clean halting deadlift
- Any exercises that keep the hips and bar (or shoulders) moving at the same rate.

MISSING POWER POSITION

There's no arguing that the power position is one of the most essential parts of Olympic weightlifting. In fact, it's the primary point I focus on when teaching. The power position ensures the bar stays close to the body, giving us more control, and allows us to optimize our power output. It's not easy for some people to produce at first.

Causes

Athletes miss the power position because they're relying on their arms more than their legs. It's more intuitive to use our arms to lift the bar, but what's more effective is the use of the hips and legs. Our arms are simply not as strong as our legs. Given that, I am a huge advocate for the triple extension. We must give the athletes exercises that allow them to focus more on the hips and legs, not the arms. Remind the athlete that they don't have to "smack" the hips into the bar, unless they "smack" the bar vertically. I agree hip contact of the bar is beneficial so long as it can be directed in the proper way; which is not out and around the body. Some athletes successfully graze the upper legs and hips with the barbell without violently impacting the bar.

Cues

- "Keep close"
- "Get into the hips"
- "Less arms, more legs"
- "Scoop" (an oldie but goodie)

Corrections

- Power position clean
- Dip clean
- Mid-hang clean pull
- Clean-high pull
- High-hang clean or clean from technique blocks

LANDING ON TOES INSTEAD OF FLAT-FOOTED

On Earth, what goes up must come down. The barbell is no different. When we jump the bar vertically, it will make its way down—and when it does, athletes need to have a solid foundation beneath them. First, let's address the width of the foot stance. I believe the pulling stance should be different than the squatting stance. The pulling stance should be narrow to allow the greatest verticality, whereas a wider stance will accommodate a comfortable squat. Next, landing flat on the feet is crucial. Striking with the toes first causes a slight delay, as it forces athletes to then roll from the balls of their feet onto their heels.

Causes

Athletes may land on their toes because it feels stronger to do so. As mentioned several times in this book, we all feel more agile and explosive on the balls of the feet. Relying on them more than the heels feels more natural, but it is not as effective. When forcing the athlete to land flat footed it will cause a solid sound of the shoes. It should be noted that excessive hang time should be avoided. In other words, the goal is to have a swift shift of the feet, or at the very least, a solid strike of the shoes with minimal distance from the floor.

Cues

- "Land flat"
- "Let me hear your feet land"
- "Land on heels" (to be used in the most dramatic of cases)

Corrections

- Dip clean
- Pause front squat
- Foot work drill (no barbell, weightless, the athlete stands then drops into a squat)

FAILURE TO TRIPLE EXTEND

Failing to triple-extend (straightening the ankles, knees, and hips) is often associated with having "muted" hips or not opening the hips all the way. Trainers often overemphasize the hips during the clean, but the issue goes far beyond that. Hips are important, yes. However, over-extending the hips may cause the bar to lose its proper path. It's less about the hips and more about the leg drive. It is feasible to "open" the hips vertically, not forward. Therefore, to fully extend the legs means to open the ankles, knees, and hips vertically. If you're visualizing this correctly, you got it, it's a jump. Unlike a jump, though, the aim is not to leave the ground excessively. The goal, rather, is to extend enough to propel the bar and move the feet in preparation for the squat. (If the athlete chooses not to squat, then he or she should at least land flat-footed.)

Causes

Athletes tend to rush their jump because the most dramatic phase of the lift is the catch. Athletes committing this error are focused on that very aspect and fail at giving the lift time to develop. The goal is to get the athlete to fully extend the legs and not shorten the jump cycle. They may be rushing to sneak under the bar. Yes, there is a risk they'll spend too much time leaving the ground with their feet. Should that occur, refer to the previous *Landing on toes* correction. In the end, we don't want to create the famous "donkey kick" which causes the athlete to waste time in the air.

Cues

- "Extend"
- "Finish"
- "Big pull"
- "Stay tall"
- "Jump longer"
- "Drop under at the last second"
- "Long legs"
- "Leg drive"

Corrections

- Tall clean
- Clean high-pull
- Clean high-pull + clean
- High-hang clean at moderately heavy weight. It will force the extension or else they'll fail at the lift.

DONKEY KICK

In the act of becoming explosive and being aggressive when receiving the barbell, athletes may develop the famous "Donkey Kick." This is when the athlete kicks the feet back while dropping under the barbell to receive it in the catch. This is a waste of valuable time and will delay the speed at which the athlete enters the squat with the barbell in the rack position.

Causes

Athletes commit this error for no other reason but to feel explosive in the catch and to hear the loud sound of their feet when receiving the barbell. The goal is for athletes to be able to extend and propel the bar (moving the feet if they choose) but land flat-footed with minimal waste of time. Remind them it's possible to create the sound with the feet leaving the ground no more than a quarter of an inch.

Cues

- "Quick feet"
- "Drop under at the last second"
- "Stay taller longer" (this will force them under with less time to waste)

Corrections

- Tall clean

- Clean from technique blocks at high-hang or waist height.
- Foot work drill (no barbell, weightless, the athlete stands then drops into a squat)

THROWING HEAD BACK

Throwing the head back during the clean can prove to ruin technique for some athletes. Yes, it's possible to do so effectively and there are a few elite lifters who get away with it. It works for them and there's little argument against them using this tactic. However, for most others, especially the beginner and intermediate practitioner, throwing the head back leads to the bar looping out and around the body instead of remaining close and vertical. It may also lead to an imbalance in the receiving phase of the lift. Some shifting back of the head is permissible. It's the excessive whipping back that should raise concern for coaches.

Causes

Athletes commit this error to feel more powerful in their jump. They have merely begun to associate an explosive pull with the whipping motion of their heads. Throwing one's head back does absolutely nothing for bar elevation. Additionally, many athletes who throw their heads back tend to close their eyes and re-open them when they receive the barbell (without even realizing it), thereby compromising their balance, as vision plays a significant role in balance. Ask your athletes to choose a location in front of them, relatively high, that they can focus on during the entirety of the lift—perhaps something with lettering. Require them to read it during the lift. Beware the first time they fix the error they may report that they feel as if they did not have a "big pull", when in fact they did.

Cues

- "Keep head straight"
- "Focus eyes in front"
- "Stare at the (chose an object in front of the athlete)"

Corrections

- Tall clean
- Establish a focal point
- Any pulling movement while focusing on maintaining a neutral head. A little pull back is okay.

KNEES IN THE WAY

Without ever being told, many new athletes do a fine job of shifting their knees back out of the path of the bar when lifting off the ground. In the instances where an athlete doesn't do it automatically and instead tracks the barbell around his or her knees, the coach should address it accordingly. This error causes the athlete to slow the speed of the bar when it should be accelerating.

Causes

Athletes committing this error actually don't know they're doing it. It comes down to body awareness. They may not know that it's possible to move the knees out of the way and still be successful with the lift. Identifying the bar tracking around the knees is an easy observation to make. Like all corrections, however, fixing it is the challenging part. This error goes back to the topic of control, mentioned earlier in the *Hips rising faster than the bar or shoulders* error. Control from the floor is extremely important. Individuals with proportionately longer legs may suffer from this error more often. This error is one of the main reasons I prefer the start position to include hips slightly higher than the height of the knees. Please refer to the Clean

Progressions section of this book for the full list of a proper set up.

Cues

- "Knees back"
- "Drive heels into the floor"
- "Knees out"
- "No toes"
- "Start on heels and stay on them throughout the lift"
- "Sweep back"

Corrections

- Clean lift-off
- Clean pull
- Low-hang clean
- Halting deadlift to knee height
- Any pulling movement, moderately heavy, where the athlete can focus on the lift from the floor to the knees

CRASHING THE BARBELL

We've all seen athletes who seem to slam the barbell onto their shoulders during the clean. It looks painful. It's an indication the athlete has disconnected from the barbell—the athlete simply extends with the barbell and then drops far below it, waiting for it to land on them. Remember, what goes up must come down. When the barbell makes its way back to the floor, the athlete needs to be ready to receive it. Slamming it is far from the most effective way.

Causes

Athletes commit this error because they're so focused on just dropping under to receive the bar that they lose contact with it. It should never be a pull up high and free-fall down under the bar. It comes down to body awareness. The moment the athlete should catch the bar isn't at the bottom of the squat. In fact, it should be "caught" at the moment the barbell has reached its highest point. That means, when it's relatively light, the athlete can rack the bar on the shoulders nearly upright and can lower into a squat, absorbing the weight. As it gets heavier, however, the barbell cannot be elevated as high, and therefore the athlete must drop under accordingly to meet the bar as it makes its way back to the floor and absorb it in the squat. This is another reason developing the squat is important to achieve maximal weight. Please see *Failing to drop under the bar* section above.

Cues

- "Smooth turnover"
- "Catch & ride"
- "Think *power clean* then lower"
- "Meet the bar"

Corrections

- Clean turnover
- Power clean + front squat
- Tempo front squat
- Pause front squat

JERK CUES & CORRECTIONS

Of the three Olympic weightlifting movements—snatch, clean, and jerk—the jerk is the most complicated to master. Ranking the lifts according to level of difficulty, the clean rates as the easiest, followed by the snatch (because of the amount of balance and mobility required), and then, lastly, the jerk. At first this may seem counterintuitive, as the barbell travels the least amount of distance in the jerk. The rack position of the clean may not be same as that of the jerk, therefore the set up for the jerk is a huge step to conquer for many. Moreover, it is precisely because the barbell in the jerk doesn't travel all that far that makes it the most technically demanding. This leaves very little room for error. Keep in mind that by definition, a jerk is any dip, drive, and re-dip (or catch) of the barbell, originating from the shoulders into the overhead position. The last part—"re-dip" or "catch"—is what separates the jerk from any other overhead movement that begins at the shoulders.

FORWARD ON TOES DURING DIP & DRIVE

Identifying an athlete distributing the weight on the balls of the feet during the dip and drive is the easiest observation to make. What's important is to identify whether he or she is doing so during the dip or on the way up on the drive. There is a difference and each should be addressed accordingly. Further, as you'll see below, the dip and drive are the most important parts of the jerk, as they are responsible for the placement of the bar, not the arms.

Causes

Athletes shift forward on either the dip, drive, or both, for the same reason they do so during the pull of the snatch or clean: they feel more powerful there. The problem, especially for the beginner or intermediate athletes, is that this puts them at risk of losing control of the bar and its path. Buckling at the knees a bit is also a common cause of this error. Remind athletes to keep their torsos vertical; they can still be powerful by staying on their heels longer. Shifting onto the toes is allowed only as a follow-through at the end of the drive, never on the dip. The athlete needs to know that once the barbell leaves the shoulders, the path of the bar cannot be altered. It will go exactly where the athlete told it to go with the drive. Perhaps if the weight is light, the athlete can manipulate it into the right place after it's left the shoulders. However, in the case of heavy, maximal lifts, the drive is fully responsible for not only propulsion, but also the direction the bar moves. Our arms are not strong enough to change the bar's course. This is why the drive is so important: it is solely responsible for where the bar ends up.

FORWARD DURING DIP

Cues

- "No toes"
- "Stay on heels down AND up"
- "Wiggle your toes inside your shoes before the jerk"
- "Knees out"

- "Chest up"
- "Stack the body"
- "Stay stacked under the bar"
- "Chin up"

Corrections

- Jerk dip hold
- Push press
- Power jerk
- Push jerk
- Behind neck jerk
- Dip & rise drill (no weight, no barbell, sliding their backs against a wall)
- Dip & rise drill (PVC pipe or dowel rod in rack position, inside a doorway, allowing the stick to grind up and down on the door frame)
- One legged squats to help strengthen the glutes

FORWARD DURING DRIVE

Cues

- "Drive off heels"
- "Drive through heels"
- "Get the bar back"
- "Stack the body"
- "Stay stacked under the bar"
- "Wiggle toes" (short for the cue used for the dip)
- "Chest up"
- "From the shoulder"
- "No arms" (over cue to minimize how much pressing the athlete might do)
- "Legs!"

Corrections

- Push press
- Power jerk
- Push jerk
- Behind neck jerk
- Dip & rise drill (no weight, no barbell, sliding their backs against a wall)
- Dip & rise drill (PVC pipe or dowel rod in rack position, inside a doorway, allowing the stick to grind up and down on the door frame)

PRESSING OUT

As indicated earlier, by definition, a jerk is any dip, drive, and re-dip (or catch) of the barbell, originating from the shoulders and ending in the overhead position. As such, athletes enjoy the feeling of their arms locking out into the overhead position without any hesitation. When there's midway tension forcing the athlete to "muscle" the bar the rest of the way by pressing it overhead, it doesn't feel as powerful and crisp. There's too much of a struggle.

Causes

Athletes commit this error because they either fail to time the lockout with the striking of the feet to the ground, or they're receiving the bar too upright and fail to lunge (or squat in the case of non-splits) low enough to accommodate the lockout. During the jerk, just like the snatch and clean, as the barbell gets heavier, athletes need the ability to move low under the bar to be successful. In order for athletes to extend the arms into an overhead lockout without hesitation, they need to think less about getting the bar up, and focus more on pushing themselves down under the barbell. We're all lucky to get a maximum jerk farther than six inches off our shoulders. For many, that is about the height of the forehead—not nearly enough to get the bar locked out with arms extended. So the athlete must embrace the fact they need to lunge down under the barbell (or squat a partial way in the case of push jerk and power jerk).

Cues

- "Lock and land"
- "Timing"
- "Drive and dive"
- "Get low"
- "Low under"
- "Leg drive"
- "Bar goes up AND back"

Corrections

- Overhead split drill (empty barbell overhead fully locked out, standing, athlete drops into split)
- Split position press
- Behind neck jerk
- Power jerk

BAR ENDS PAST THE FRONTAL PLANE

In a situation where the barbell has proper height, the athlete lowers sufficiently enough to lock their arms out, but the barbell remains in front, it is difficult to hold. This is an indicator that the bar is being propelled in the wrong direction.

Causes

Athletes commit this error because they don't yet know how to deliver the barbell behind their head in the locked out position. They are focusing so much on barbell elevation they neglect its path. It's a two-part equation: propulsion and direction. I'm not a fan of using the cue "straight up", because—if taken literally—this would not place the bar in the proper position. Straight up from the shoulders would actually make the bar feel forward. The bar should go up and back together. Not only do we want elevation, we want direction as well, and, as stated previously, the time for it to occur is during the drive—not after it's left the shoulders.

Cues

- "From the shoulders"
- "No pushing with arms"
- "Drive the bar up and back"
- "Behind the ears"
- "Behind the head"

Corrections

- Behind neck split position press
- Behind neck jerk
- Behind neck press
- Behind neck push press
- Behind neck push jerk/power jerk

SPLIT POSITION IMBALANCE, INCONSISTENCIES OR DISCOMFORT

For those who split jerk, mastering proper stance, balance, consistency and comfort can be challenging. Sometimes there's a loss of balance and other times the feet don't land in the exact same spot each time. There are ways around this, but first athletes must ensure they're using the correct front and rear foot stance (Please refer to the Jerk Progressions of this book for proper determination of footing). There may also be mobility issues in the shoulders, preventing them from ever finding a comfortable stance. This lack of flexibility must be addressed outside of training in addition to drill work.

Causes

Athletes committing this error are simply not yet comfortable with their stance. In order to become so, they must find their best front foot and back leg and gain stability. Once the proper footing is established, the way to become comfortable is through many repetitions of low weight or through non-weight-bearing exercises. It's not a matter of getting strong in the position, although that will come. It's a matter of being comfortable and consistent. This is a neurological response and the timing must be practiced.

Cues

- "Feet hit together"
- "Wide stance" (for those who keep their feet in line)
- "No tight roping"

Corrections

- Foot work drill (no weight, no barbell, standing and dropping into the split stance)
- Split position press
- Overhead split drills

ONE FOOT STRIKES BEFORE THE OTHER IN THE SPLIT JERK

Most often, when one foot strikes the floor first, it's the rear foot. During real time speed, the athlete should feel—and the coach should observe what appears to be—both feet striking the floor simultaneously. Let me stress that this is a real-time analysis. In slow motion, or frame by frame, almost all of us actually strike the back foot first. If this is visible during live speed, it means it's excessive. The moment we connect with the ground, we're applying force. If it appears the athlete is striking simultaneously, then it's safe to say the force is being applied equally. However, if in live motion there's clearly a distinction between the feet, then there is unequal distribution of the weight, and the timing is ruined. This could potentially cause the body to push forward or backward when we want it to be directly under the bar.

Causes

Athletes commit this error because they rush to their dominant leg to apply force against the floor. In most cases, when one foot strikes the floor before the other, the dominant leg is the culprit. The floor is our friend in weightlifting, and when we're connected to it we feel secure. Of all split problems, this should be the easiest to fix. It's important to identify which foot is striking first and address that leg specifically. If we assume the foot that strikes first is attached to the dominant leg, we cannot assume that the dominant leg should become the front foot. Many successful weightlifters use their dominant leg as their rear foot. In all split jerks, the front leg is the anchor, and the rear leg is the control that stabilizes us and helps with lunging lower as necessary.

Cues

- "Simultaneous"
- "Feet react together"
- "Front foot out farther" (In the cases it's the leg striking first. This will delay its contact to the ground)
- "Back leg longer" (In the case it's the leg striking first. This will delay its contact to the ground.)

Corrections

- Foot work drill (no weight, no barbell, standing and dropping into the split stance)
- Split position press
- Overhead split drills
- Split holds

LOSING CONTACT WITH THE BAR DURING THE DIP & DRIVE

Many trainers encourage athletes to initiate the jerk (dip & drive) as quickly as possible. I am not a fan of doing so. This puts the athlete at risk of losing contact with the bar. That is, as previously stated, we want full contact of the bar from one shoulder to the opposite shoulder. If an athlete dips too quickly, the shoulders will lose the connection and the bar is left to drop on its own. I am a big believer in having constant tension with the barbell in all lifts associated with Olympic weightlifting. The momentary loss of tension causes a violent crash when the athlete then drives up against the bar. It is better to encourage the athlete to initiate the jerk with control, letting the bar take them down into the dip. What has to be quick then is the reversal of direction to propel the barbell upwards.

Causes

The athlete tries to be as fast as possible in order to create vertical propulsion of the barbell. It's not the same as saying the athlete is rushing the movement, however. What we're saying is they are trying to create such speed on the bar that they lose the connection with it and in turn cause the barbell to rattle or bounce on the shoulder as opposed to creating a smooth transfer of energy.

Cues

- "Let the bar take you down"
- "Control"
- "Control dip, drive up hard"
- "Slow down, fast up"
- "Control dip"

Corrections

- Push press
- Dip hold
- Power jerk

DRILLS

Drills are exercises that help the athlete develop certain abilities, such as speed, timing of the movements, and technique. Drills are not always associated with only proper form, but can develop controlled power. Below is a list of the most common drills for three basic goals: speed, timing and the transition.

Videos of the following drills are available online:

http://camargo.catalystathletics.com

Username: camargo
Password: corrections

SPEED

Everyone wants to be fast with the barbell. It's beneficial to be explosive and have quick hips, for example, but it does no good if the athlete lacks bar control. As mentioned earlier in this book, the number one priority when learning the Olympic weightlifting movements is controlling the path of the bar. Speed and explosiveness will come later down the line when bar control has been achieved consistently. What makes a lift appear fast isn't the pull but rather the catch. This applies to the snatch, clean, jerk. Study any elite weightlifter and you'll notice the pull is relatively slow. It's when the bar becomes weightless and the lifter moves under it that the lift is fast as lightening. With that in mind, all speed drills are aimed at developing the catch.

SNATCH

- Snatch balance
- Drop snatch
- Dip snatch
- Snatch Turnover

CLEAN

- Clean turnover
- Dip clean
- High-hang power clean

JERK

- Power jerk
- Split position foot work drill
- Split position press (punching the lockout into place)

There is one other way to develop speed with the lifts and it's more about the approach to all exercises performed in the gym. Athletes can't expect to be fast if they are executing movements slowly. All eccentric (negative) portions of an exercise should be done with control; however, the concentric portion should be executed with as much effort as possible—every rep of every set, each and every day. Example: In the back squat, move downward with control, but on the way up, drive up as fast as possible. The same can be applied to other exercises such as the RDL (Romanian deadlift), push press, and bench press. Even if the load is increased and the speed isn't as visible as when it was light, the effort behind it will still be training the proper muscle fibers to develop speed. Attacking these accessory exercises will transfer to the snatch, clean, and jerk.

TIMING

Timing differs from speed in that it refers to the ability to move the body while the bar is weightless momentarily before beginning to fall again with gravity. An example would be locking out the arms in the overhead position at the same time the feet split in a jerk. Another would be smoothly receiving the barbell onto the shoulders while squatting during a clean. Timing is important because it allows athletes to better optimize their functional stability. Failure to have proper timing can challenge steadiness and slow the lifter down.

SNATCH

- Dip snatch
- Power snatch (Continue into overhead squat without standing first after catch)
- Power position snatch
- Snatch balance

CLEAN

- Dip clean
- Power position clean
- Power clean pause

JERK

- Overhead split foot work drill
- Power jerk
- Behind neck jerk

Mastered timing is very impressive to look at. The amount of control demonstrated by the athlete is advanced and develops huge confidence. The word "timing" can also be used as a cue for athletes who have a sense of it.

TRANSITION

Weightlifting tradition breaks the extension of the snatch and clean into three parts: The first pull, the transition, and the second pull. Early on in the learning process it becomes easy to lift the bar from the ground (first pull) and it's easy to jump into the catch (second pull). What is often the challenge is connecting the two, the part where we keep the bar moving past the knees into the power position, better known as the "transition." In the case where an athlete can't quite "scoop" the bar, these drills have done wonders for me as a coach.

SNATCH

- Any variation of snatch from technique blocks where the bar rests above the knees
- Mid-hang snatch
- Mid-hang snatch pull
- Mid-hang snatch high-pull
- Moving through transition with an empty bar, at controlled speed
- Snatch-grip lift-off

CLEAN

- Any variation of the clean from technique blocks where the bar rests above the knees

- Mid-hang clean
- Mid-hang clean pull
- Mid-hang clean high-pull
- Moving through transition with an empty bar, at controlled speed
- Clean-grip lift-off (illustrated with snatch grip)

As mentioned earlier in the book, the power position is the most vital part of the Olympic weightlifting movements (see the Snatch Progressions chapter). Getting into it after lifting the bar from the floor, at maximal velocity, is challenging for many beginning and intermediate lifters. It's a motor skill that isn't natural for people and there must be an emphasis on it by the coach. I use additional cues for those struggling with the transition, such as "into the hips" (not to mean smack the hips with the bar, only directing the athlete to keep the bar close), "shift to heels", "no arms", and "mirror the body" (directing the athlete to keep the bar along the body from start to finish).

Daniel Camargo is a 24-year veteran of Olympic Weightlifting. He learned the snatch and clean & jerk at age 12 and has never left the sport. As an athlete, Camargo represented the USA in nine international competitions and set three Junior American Records. At 21 years old, which was his final competition year, and weighing 83 kg (182.6 lbs.), Camargo lifted 152.5 kg (334 lbs) in the snatch and 180 kg (396 lbs) in the clean & jerk, a Junior American Record. He was trained by some of the very best US coaches and has since risen to the same level of coaching.

Within a year after retiring from competition, Camargo began his coaching career. As a head coach, Camargo has produced several State, Collegiate and National Champions. Successfully passing the necessary levels of coaching certifications, along with athlete production, Camargo is currently a USA Weightlifting International Level Coach. In 2008, Camargo was elected President of the Florida Weightlifting Federation and is still in office. He has served the weightlifting community in his home state of Florida since beginning in 2004 as the vice president.

Camargo has been given several assignments by USA Weightlifting as a coach for Team USA, one of which was the job of Team Leader and Coach for the Junior World Championships, held in Romania in 2009. There he led the team for 10 days as USA's best junior athletes competed in the very prestigious championship tournament. Coach Camargo's experience and education has made him one of the most well-known coaches in the sport of Olympic weightlifting. He is also the owner of Altamonte Crossfit, near Orlando, Florida, recognized as a USA Weightlifting Regional Training Center, actively coaches both weightlifters and CrossFit competitors, and travels frequently conducting seminars.

Camargo is known for his enthusiasm, passion, and extensive knowledge about Olympic weightlifting. He expresses it all between his daily programming of athletes, at competitions, through his seminars, as a business owner, and as a USA Weightlifting Coaching Certification Instructor. You can find more about Coach Camargo and his philosophies on his website www.olyconcepts.com.